Mother Remembers

For My Daughter

It is only with the heart that one can see rightly;
what is essential is invisible to the eye.

ANTOINE DE SAINT-EXUPÈRY

Mother Remembers
For My Daughter

EDITED BY CASSANDRA CASE

DESIGNED BY FABIA WARGIN DESIGN

STERLING PUBLISHING CO., INC.

Memory is the diary
we all carry about with us.

OSCAR WILDE

Published by Sterling Publishing Company, Inc.
387 Park Avenue South, New York, NY 10016
Printed in China

STERLING ISBN 0-8069-9141-0

Gathered together for:

. . . .

Recall it as often as you wish,
a happy memory never wears out.

LIBBIE FUDIM

With love from:

. . . .

Contents

Dear Daughter, This is for you, because...

We are shaped and fashioned by what we love.

JOHANN WOLFGANG VON GOETHE

About Your Mother...Me

My given names ....

....

My nicknames ....

....

Date of my birth ....

....

Place of my birth ....

....

In search of my mother's garden I found my own.

ALICE WALKER

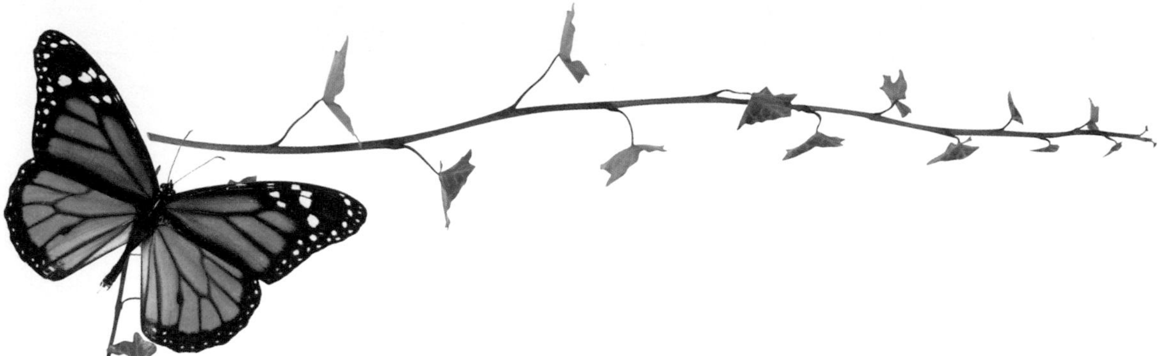

Pictures of Me

When I stopped seeing my mother with the eyes of a child,
I saw the woman who helped me give birth to myself.

NANCY FRIDAY

I Remember My Mother and Father

(your grandmother and grandfather)

What you called your grandmother and grandfather

Other things may change us,
but we start and end with family.

ANTHONY BRANDT

What I Remember About My Grandparents

(your great grandparents) and other people who cared for me when I was little

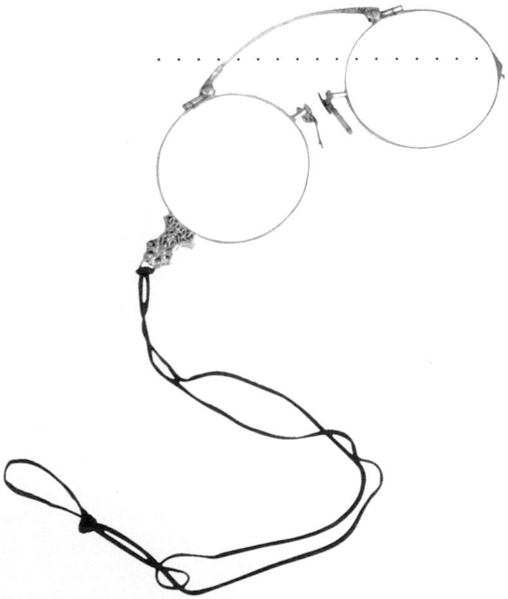

Only love can be divided endlessly and still not diminish.

ANNE MORROW LINDBERGH

When I Was Little

My earliest memories

My favorite memories

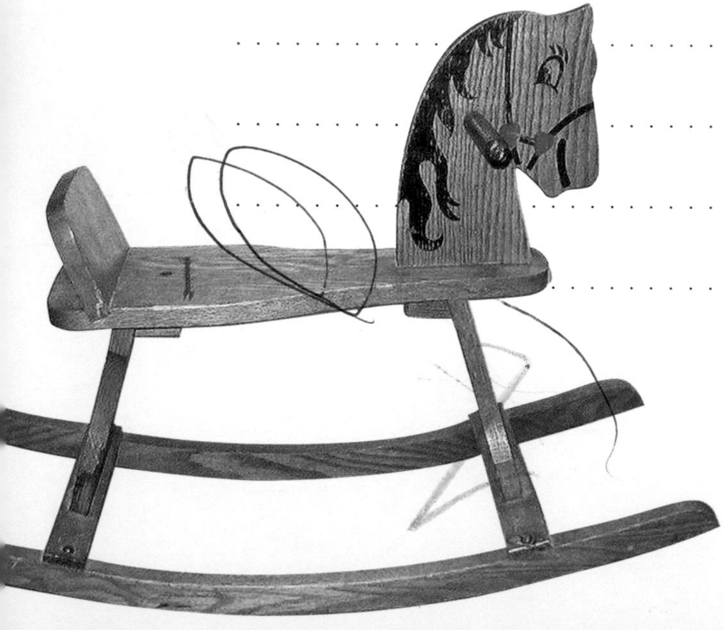

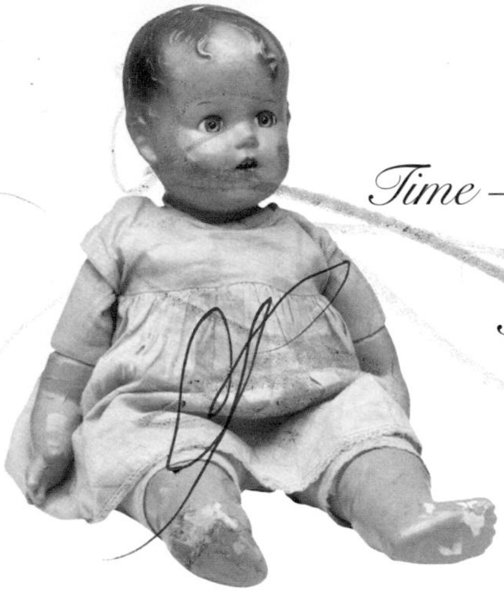

Time – our youth – it never really goes,
does it?
It is all held in our minds.

HELEN HOOVEN SANTMYER

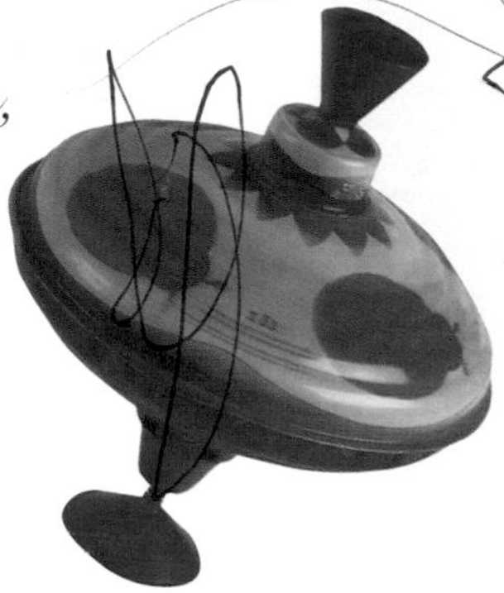

My favorite toys

Pictures of My Family

The Place Where I Grew Up

Home is not a structure, but something in your heart.

AMERICAN PROVERB

What We Did in Summer

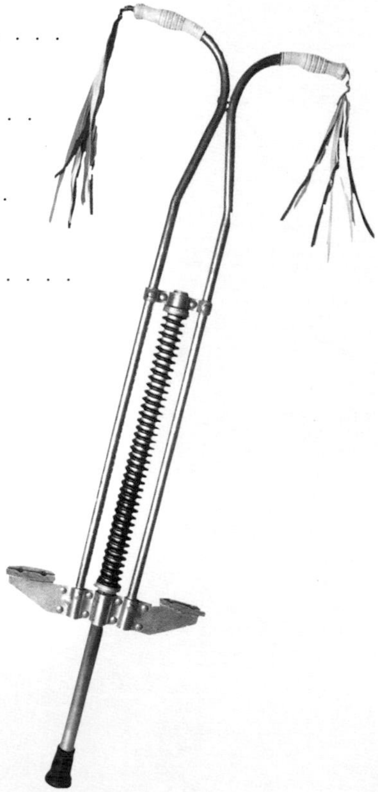

Kids I Played With

Their names and who they were to me

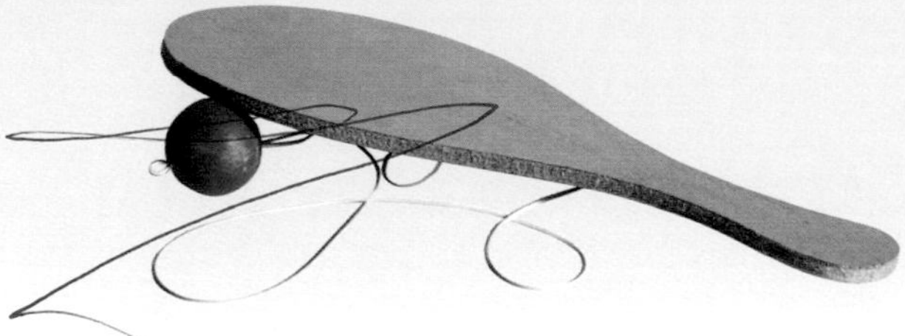

Our favorite things to do

To live is so startling
it leaves little time for anything else.

EMILY DICKINSON

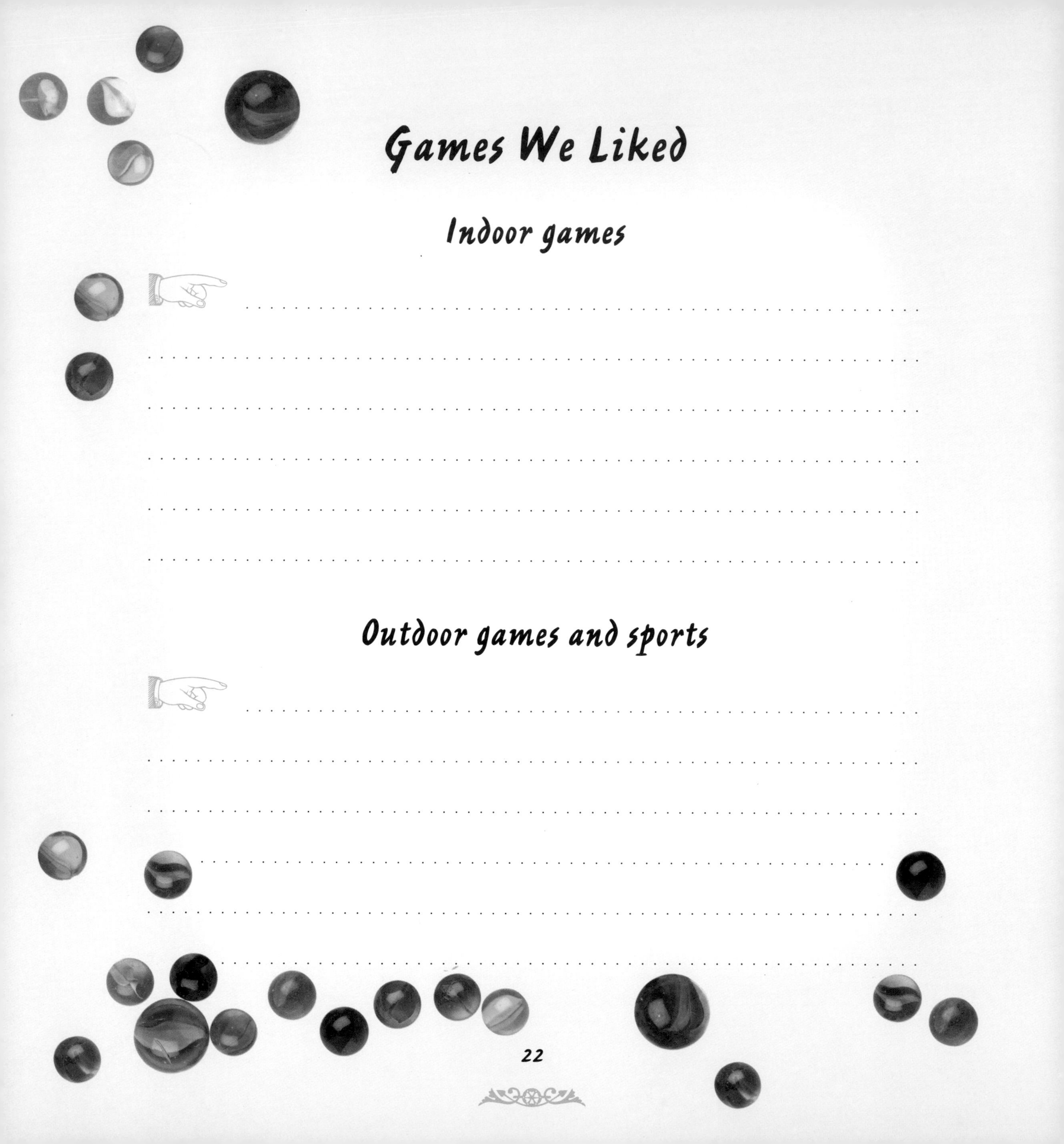

Games We Liked

Indoor games

Outdoor games and sports

Make-believe

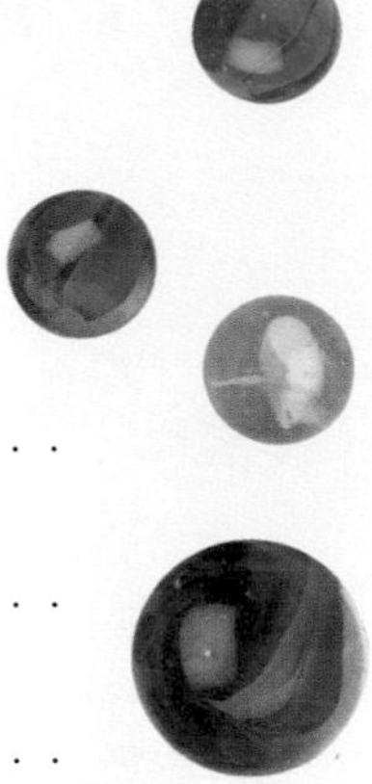

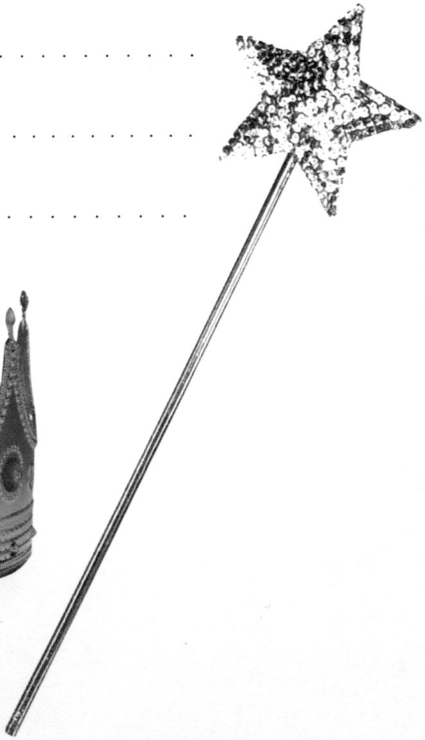

Pets I Had

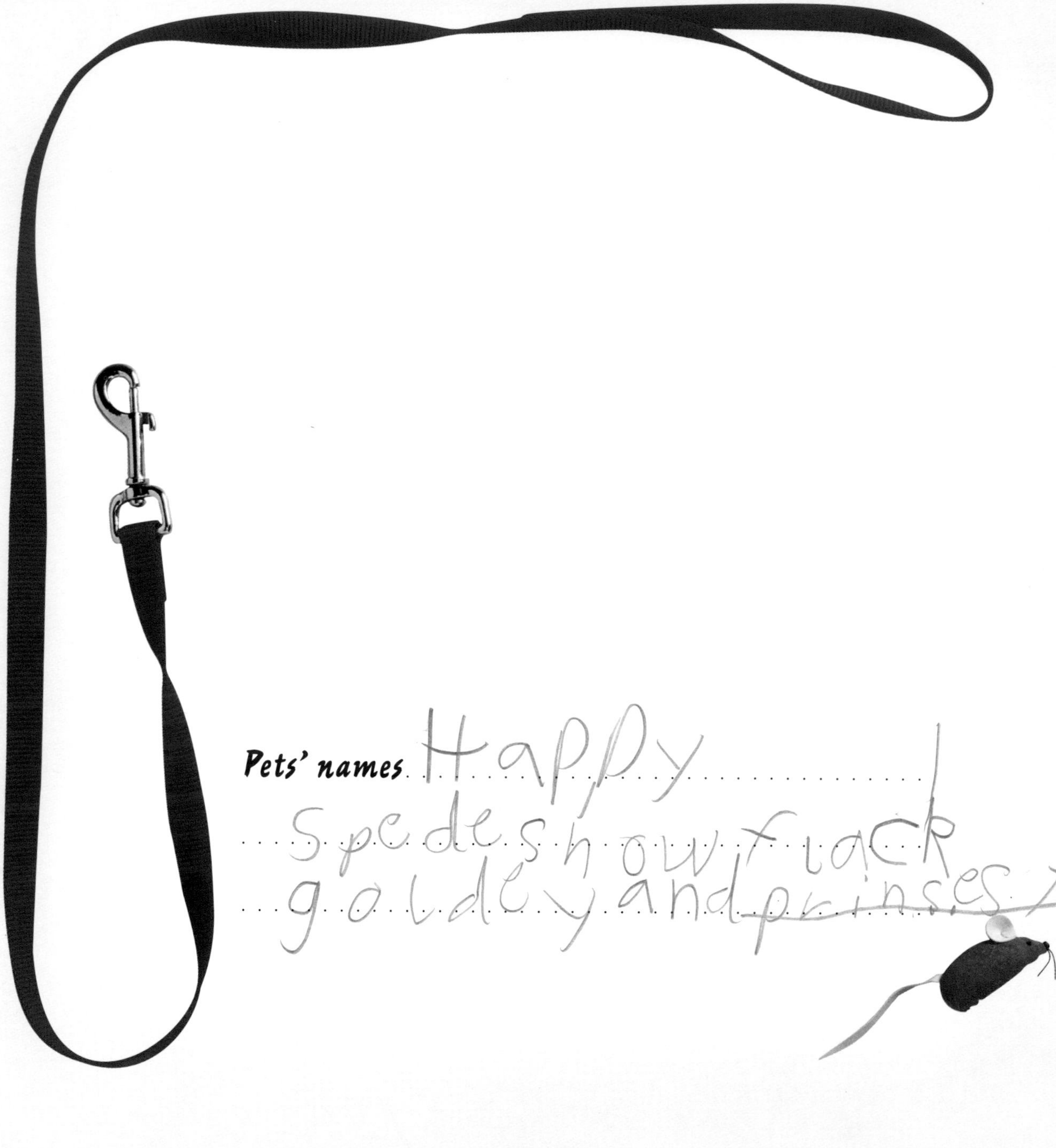

Pets' names Happy

Spedeshowfiack

goldey and prinses ALay

Pets I Wanted

☞ a snack abunny

Reasons I couldn't have them

☞ snack becus my mom dose not like them and It prezents saten.

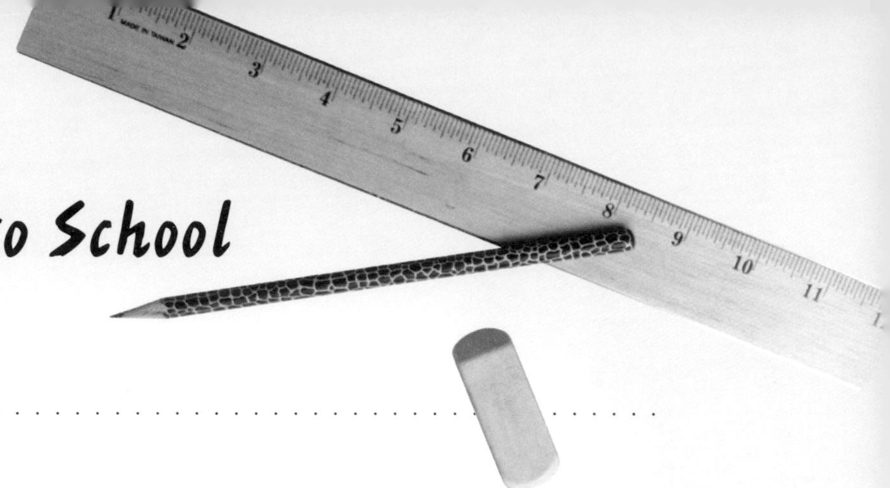

Off to School

Schools I went to

How I got to school

Memorable teachers

My school friends

Me as a Teenager

My room

My girlfriends

My boyfriends

(or guys I had a crush on)

What We Thought Was "In"

The music we listened to

Styles we liked to wear

Cars we drove

Entertainment

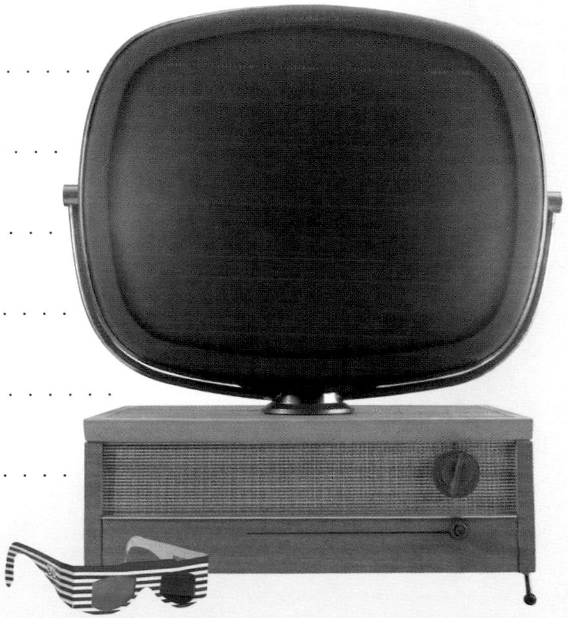

Firsts and Funnies

First job

First car

First love

First time on my own

Funny stories

What I Did When I Finished High School

Where I went

Special things I did

STATE

Some of My Favorite People

Favorite Times in My Life

How I Met Your Father

What it was that I liked about him

Places we went together

How he proposed

Your Maternal Family Tree

YOUR MOTHER

....
Name

....
Date of birth

....
Place of birth

YOUR GRANDMOTHER

....
Name

....
Date of birth

....
Place of birth

YOUR GRANDFATHER

....
Name

....
Date of birth

....
Place of birth

Your grandmother's Mother

....

....

Your grandmother's Father

....

....

Your grandfather's Mother

....

....

Your grandfather's Father

....

....

Your grandmother's Grandmother

....

....

Your grandmother's Grandfather

....

....

Your grandfather's Grandmother

....

....

Your grandfather's Grandfather

....

....

Your Paternal Family Tree

YOUR FATHER

....
Name

....
Date of birth

....
Place of birth

YOUR GRANDMOTHER

....
Name

....
Date of birth

....
Place of birth

YOUR GRANDFATHER

....
Name

....
Date of birth

....
Place of birth

Your grandmother's Mother

....

....

Your grandmother's Father

....

....

Your grandfather's Mother

....

....

Your grandfather's Father

....

....

Your grandmother's Grandmother

....

....

Your grandmother's Grandfather

....

....

Your grandfather's Grandmother

....

....

Your grandfather's Grandfather

....

....

Our Wedding

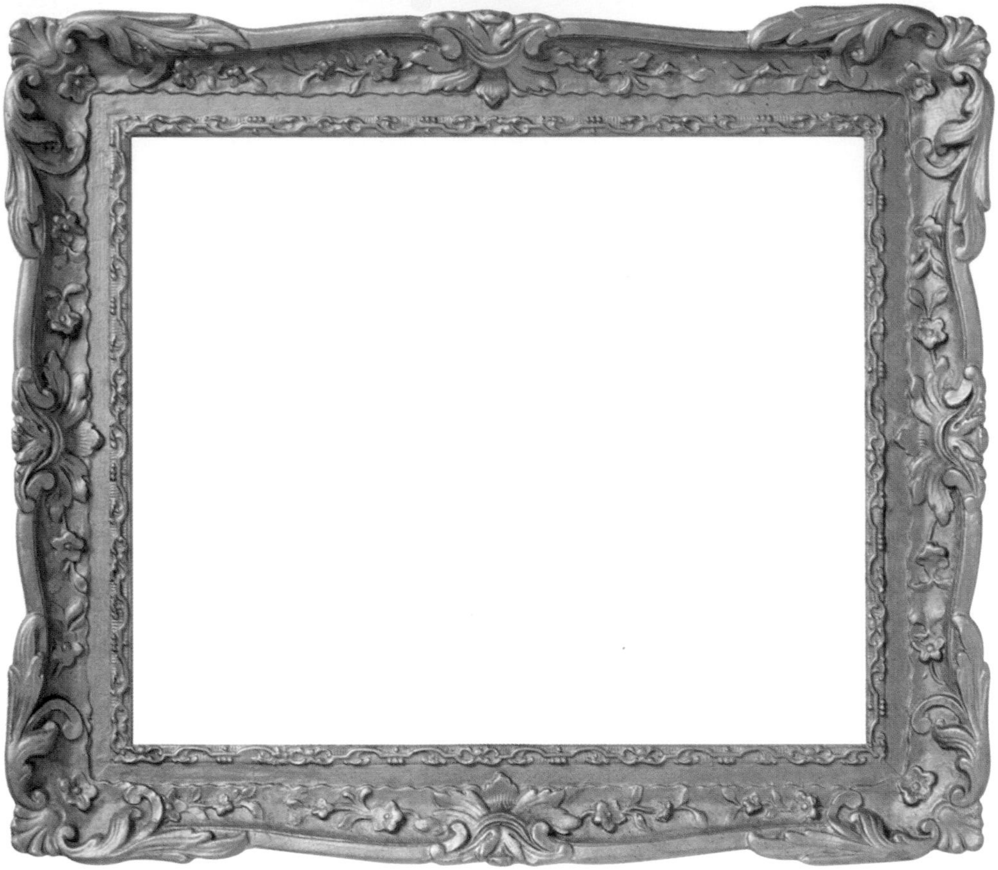

The day. . . . .

The time. . . . .

The place . . . .

The party we had

Where we went for our honeymoon

When I Knew You Were on the Way

How I felt

It is a feeling of intimacy and exclusiveness…
a warm, lazy, intimate gaiety.

DORIS LESSING

Whom we told first

When You Were Born

Date . . . .

Time . . . .

Place . . . .

Your weight and length . . . .

I looked at this tiny, perfect creature
and it was as though a light switch had been turned on.
A great rush of love, mother love, flooded out of me.

MADELEINE L'ENGLE

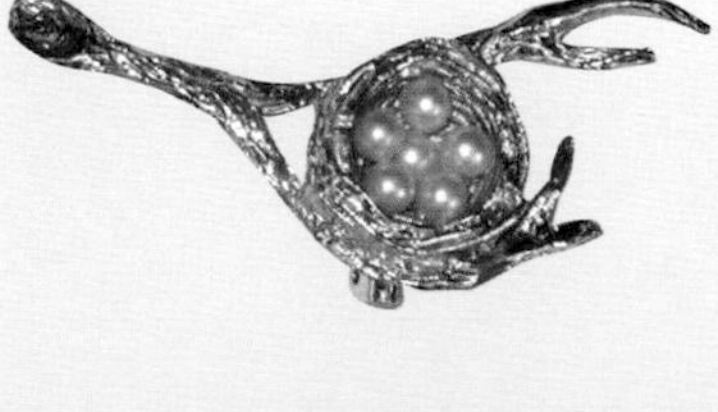

You!

Your name . . . .

The meaning of your name . . . .

. . . .

. . . .

How we decided on your name . . . .

. . . .

. . . .

Other names we thought about . . . .

. . . .

. . . .

Compliments you received

Gifts you received

When We Brought You Home

Your first days in the family

There is nothing more thrilling in this world,
I think, than having a child that is yours,
and yet is mysteriously a stranger.

AGATHA CHRISTIE

More Photos of You!

O young thing, your mother's lovely armful!
How sweet the fragrance of your body!

EURIPIDES

Things I Wanted To Tell You

How I felt

What your father did

Things you did

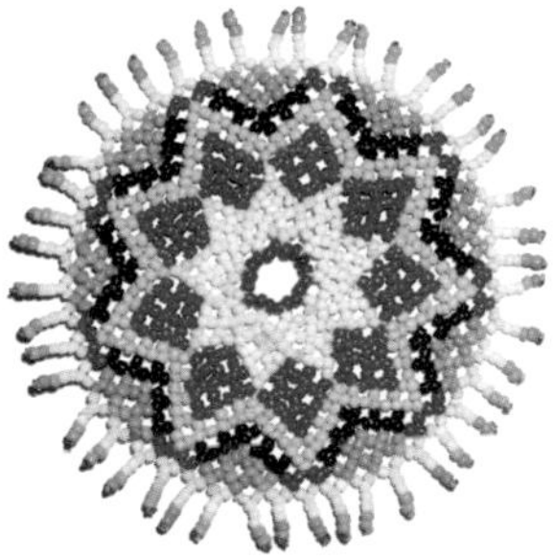

My daughter's birth was the incomparable gift
of seeing the world at quite a different angle than before
and judging it by standards that would apply
far beyond my natural life.

ALICE WALKER

Memorable Moments

When you first smiled . . . .

. . . .

When you first rolled over by yourself . . . .

. . . .

Your first solid food . . . .

. . . .

Your favorite foods . . . .

. . . .

When you first stood up ....

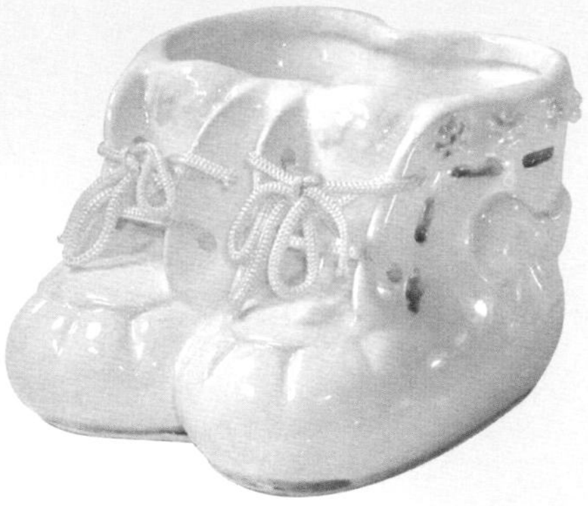

....

Your first birthday party ....

....

When you first walked by yourself ....

....

Your first words ....

....

Sleepytime

Bedtime rituals

When you woke up at night

The only thing worth stealing is a kiss from a sleeping child.

JOE HOULDSWORTH

Music

First songs you liked me to sing

First songs you sang

Music you responded to

How you responded

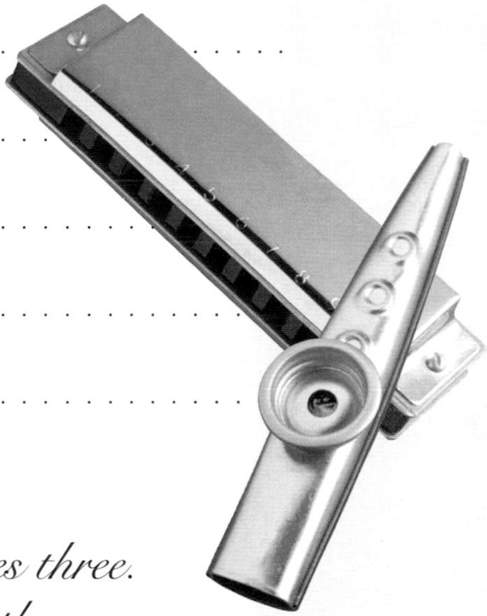

Over in the meadow in a hole in a tree
Lived an old mother bluebird and her little birdies three.
"Sing!" said the mother; "We sing!" said the three.
So they sang and were glad in a hole in the tree.

OLIVE A. WADSWORTH

Books, Toys and TV

There is no frigate like a book to take us lands away.

EMILY DICKINSON

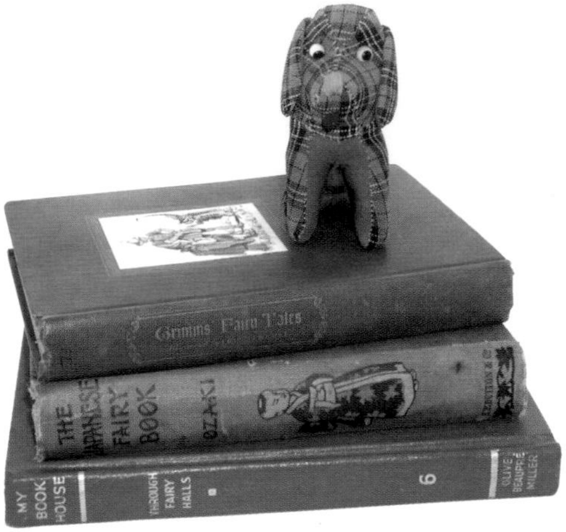

Favorite books

Favorite TV programs and videos

Favorite toys

Growing Up ...

I have seen a young girl walk across a room,
intent on her intense errand, and it was like seeing a voice
become visible, as if not her tongue but her motion said,
"I will do this for my life."

PAUL ENGLE

Favorite Games, Indoors and Out

Whom you played with

School

A B C D E F G
Z H
Y I
X J
W K
V L
U M
T S R Q P O N

Your first day at school

. . . .

. . . .

. . . .

. . . .

New friends

Favorite teachers

After school activities

Stages and Milestones

Things you did

Things you said

Some thoughts and feelings I had

Things We Did Together

That is the best – to laugh with someone because you both think the same things are funny.

GLORIA VANDERBILT

Places We Went

The perfect journey is circular –
the joy of departure and the joy of return.

DINO BASILI

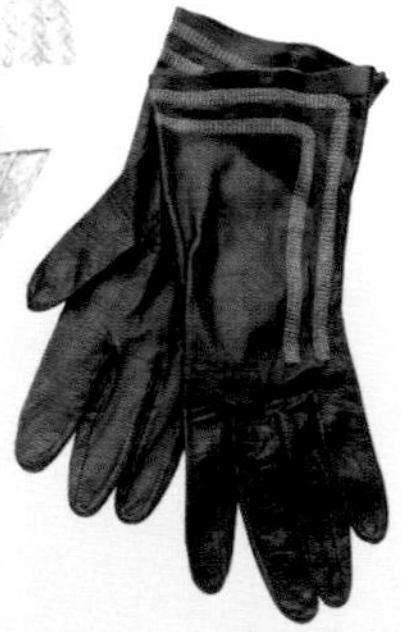

SF27341
CUNARD WHITE STAR TO EUROPE
CUNARD WHITE STAR LINE
21
Hotel
NATIONAL
MUENCHEN
WANTED

Clippings, Souvenirs and Mementos

SCRAP
BOOK

Thoughts to Hold on To

Never grow a wishbone, daughter, where your backbone ought to be.

CLEMENTINE PADDLEFORD

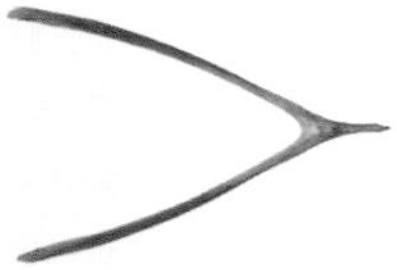

Life is change. Growth is optional. Choose wisely.

KAREN KAISER

You must do the thing you think you cannot do.

ELEANOR ROOSEVELT

Life begets life. Energy creates energy.
It is by spending oneself that one becomes rich.

SARAH BERNHARDT

Hopes, Wishes and Prayers for You, My Daughter

Be happy. It is a way of being wise.

COLETTE

Don't be afraid of the space between your dreams and reality. If you can dream it, you can make it so.

BELVA DAVIS